The Good Time Girls:
Voices from Beyond
the Grave

Poems by
Gail Marshall

The Good Time Girls: Voices From Beyond the Grave: Poems by
Gail Marshall
©2019 Gail Marshall

ISBN 979-8-60-165554-5

Cover design: Victor Massetti, victormassettidesign.com
Book interior design: Jeff Hirsch

The Good Time Girls:
Voices from Beyond the Grave

Gail Marshall

Pisces Sun Press
St. Louis, MO

Table of Contents

Part One

Part Two

Part One

Scheherazade

Each day I saw my father the grand vizier
weeping in our garden where roses, hyacinths
bloomed all year. Herbs, oranges,
lemons, grapes were ours for the taking.
So his sorrow could not be because the lives
of my sister Dinarzade and I were poor.

I watched. I listened when no one
was aware. I heard whispers, rumors
about Sultan Schahriar. I learned
about the horrible death of the Sultan's wife,
murdered when he discovered
her treachery, lying with other men. I heard
he decided he could not trust women
so each night chose a beautiful young girl
to sleep with, then ordered my father to kill her.

One day, when my father was walking in the garden,
bending to stroke a rose, I dared approach him.
"Father," I said, "I know about your sorrow
and I have a plan."

Persephone

The surge of joy, the thrill of lust,
weren't my fault. Love overcame me.
But it's my fault always. That's how she tells the story.
Mothers are all alike: nag, nag, nag.
So the earth is plunged in cold and misery
half the year and it is my fault.

Sitting in the agora, I wanted
to hear more besides, "Wash your chiton;
be sure to rub olive oil into your skin.
Did you do this? Don't do that,
people will talk. Walk modestly,
guard your eyes, drink little wine."

So when he appeared and treated me like a goddess,
promised caresses, nights of ecstasy, a palace of my own,
freedom to be myself and his, only his,
why wouldn't I follow him?

It was her fault. She had to call out, one last time,
and when I turned to tell her I was finally free
of her following me everywhere, it happened.
He beckoned and I went gladly.

She got a lonely life half the year
and I got nights I never knew could happen,
days beneath the soft blanket of the earth
where I am his one and only.
Tell them all to stop complaining
about a few months of cold and rain.

Calypso

You plucked the luscious grapes that hung
around my cave. We swam in cooling streams
that flowed like love. I remember when you
mounted me in those streams and I quivered in your arms.

But you cried, you mourned, missing a wife
not seen in years, who cannot match my charms
or ardor, and must have forgotten you long ago.

Go. I'll give you trees' trunks
from my splendid forest where we whiled
away sunlit days and windy nights.
Make a raft, take my wine, some clothes.

You will never again be the man you were when in my arms,
Odysseus.

Demeter

Every day in the marketplace they cluck,
"If only she had made her daughter behave,
watched where she was going—to the agora,
the vineyards, if she had supervised the tending of herbs
and the rinsing of amphorae as I always did
with my Daphne and my Iris."

Good ladies, when gods swoop in and entice
young maidens, when they woo your daughters
by promising long nights of love,
you'll learn the hard way there's a wildness in the blood,
especially when the earth bursts forth with blossoms
and birds sing, "Take love while you may."
Your daughters will creep away through the fields
seeking love without a thought of you.

Eve

In the beginning
the noise was awful.
The Big Voice
hovered in the clouds,
booming, cranky.
"Watch where you walk among the willows.
Don't swat the bees. Stop petting the lions."

And if that weren't enough, the snake
always watched me when I washed in the river,
flicking his forked tongue and leering, yes, leering!

The Bumpkin who followed me everywhere
was no better, mumbling, stammering,
stroking his rib cage and nattering
on and on about the rules.

It put me off my food,
wondering if eating raspberries
or the new peas was allowed.

One day I told him, "Mind what you say to me
or I'll set the snake on you."
He laughed.

He isn't laughing now.
But I'm not laughing either with two kids
who can't get along and the useless sod
moans and groans about working,
sweat on his brow as he tries to till the soil,
then talks all night about the good old days.

Gertrude, Queen of Denmark

One day I saw Claudius as I had never seen him.
At that moment my life changed. I desired him.
My body was throbbing as I turned away.
Many nights, after King Hamlet had his way with me,
I closed my eyes and imagined Claudius
slowly undressing me, kissing my neck,
my breasts, working his way down my body,
quivering with longing.
A wife carrying burdens of statehood,
offering hospitality to courtiers at our table,
I had forgotten what men and women can give one another.

"No more," I thought. "In the years left to me I must be a partner
in pleasure. Arouse a man with my body and spirit.
Be engulfed in the act of passion I've made myself forget."
One day, when his hand held mine it lingered.
From that moment he was mine and I was his. It needed
the dispatch of King Hamlet, I know not how;
the ceremonies to unite us, not soon enough for me,
for us to share a rightful bed, nights of loving embraces
for me to become the woman I was meant to be.

Not knowing a woman's desires, my son despised me.
He thought me a traitor. I own he was right. But I had to obey
my body, heart, and will. A boy
cannot know love unless he knows it for himself.

Instead of hating me he should have given Ophelia
the love I sought and won. I offer no apology.

Penelope

Stupid fools, thinking one of them could win me.
Daily they sat talking of their vineyards
or ships and slaves, waiting for me to cast a longing look
at one of them.
But I held my breath in fear
one might grab me and carry me away.
I sang of the days long ago, before the war,
as I wove, picking threads, plying the needle,
waiting all the while for my love
to leave that charnel house and hurry home.

Damn you, Odysseus, telling a harlot
tales of valor while I languished alone and afraid.
Caress and fondle me all night.
Let's go to the tavernas or the campfires,
and get love's licks in.

Molly Bloom

Of course I said yes when he proposed.
Yes was all I needed to say.
Yes was my surrender.
Yes to feeling him embrace me,
to his kisses, soft and warm
and yes to the rapture none but I have ever known.
I'd say "Yes" if he asked
and "Yes, yes," if he roused
and slid into me, enslaving me.

Odette

Swann was such a strange man!
Creeping around my house
at night, peering in my windows,
looking for a secret lover!

Twiddling his thumbs
at boring dinner parties,
waiting for the evening to end
so he could take me home in his carriage.

As if no one knew we were lovers,
that he adored me, bought me
anything I desired, sent flowers and jewels
even though he was careful of his money.

I longed for a maison in a good district
but he withheld money just as he withheld himself.
Was his refusal a warning to me
that his love wasn't lasting?

Swann loved no one but Swann.
I could have loved him
but no one mattered more to Swann
than Swann.

Part Two

Grendel's Modor

When they sit around their fires, telling the story,
I am called wretch, monster, demon,
troll, roaming slaughter spirit, valkyrie…
I have no name. Let it be.

Sick at heart, I knew Grendel could not win.
He cared not. I could not hold him back.
Too eager to do battle
he rushed toward his death.
As I had foretold,
so it was.

I grieved.
What mother wouldn't? On fire to avenge,
burrowed in a cave, I lay in wait.
I knew Beowulf would attack.
He did.

He wrestled me. I pinned him,
holding him down with all I had.
He grabbed a splendid sword, who wouldn't want
to die by such a sword? I tried to breathe,
was overcome. I died.
I almost won.

Cleopatra

There's no respect in this stinking pit of swirling smoke.
I'm a goddess. Prayers were offered in my name,
offerings laid upon altars, animals sacrificed.

No one knows who I am or bows down to me,
the woman whom men bedded with sweet words,
who feared my moods, worshipped my body.

I had a forest cut down and built the Romans war ships.
I commanded an army, dispensed justice,
solaced Caesar when he was a crude general.
I showed Antony how a civilized woman lives,
fed him roast pig and sea urchins while we sat
on a floor strewn with roses.

In that world the sweet smells of flowers
filled my palaces; odors of herb gardens
calmed me, whiffs of salty air from the sea delighted.
Jewels—pearls, topaz, lapis, emeralds, amethyst—
garlanded me; soft linen enfolded my skin
massaged with myrrh, lily, cardamom.

I feasted on dates, figs, grapes, partridge and quail.
All was light and beauty and ceremony.
I, who once drove men to frenzy,
stand in this fiery cauldron by myself.

Lady Macbeth

The raven's croak outside the castle walls
chilled me. I felt the sting of death,
my hands growing cold, heartbeat slowing,
but I wanted victory, Macbeth rising,
Duncan falling.

Macbeth, weakly wavering,
withdrew from his desire to drive
the sword and I had to man him again
until he screwed his courage for the deed.

The owl's cry, "Fall, die,"
stiffened my spirits, emboldened Macbeth
who slashed in a frenzy of ambition.
I, fearing nothing, smeared blood
where it told a tale absolving us.

But while the witches conjured visions
murder followed murder,
Macbeth, unsettled,
unleashing deaths. I wandered, bewitched,
was purged and died, alas. Not there
when Macduff swung the fateful sword.

Mrs. Robinson

It's time for a martini
but there's no drinks
in this god-awful place.

No cigarettes, no strip poker,
no spa manicures
and the young guys are slobs.

As for the older guys,
forget it. They're losers,
look like used-car salesmen.

I long to get my hands on
a stud, a guy with moxie.
Someone who'd tear off my clothes in a minute.

Oh, and my clothes, forget it!
Dreary gray, dark brown, black
looking like something left out in the rain.

I'd climb over a fence,
hitch a ride, but there's no fence,
no road, just acres of smoking muck.

I'm at my wit's end.
Got to get out of here.
Maybe one of the guys knows where the exit is.

Can't stay in this shit hole another minute.

Helen

King Menelaus lay with all the tarts
and sluts, ladling
the new wine, his horny hands
groping, thrusting himself
wherever led by his will and lust.

Stretching his long arms,
he trapped me. Like an octopus,
he wound himself around me,
gripping, licking, nipping
until he conquered me.

Thank Zeus, those ships shuddered ashore.
Kings, swordsmen and the trash of war
came tumbling from the sea
and bundled me away.
I was a prize, an exotic souvenir,
and loved the turmoil my arrival caused,

glancing, flirting, sighing
at all the bronzed young men.
I gave myself to any and all,
fool that I was.
Ladies, learn from this empty shell.

Beware of kings.
Men work their will,
then, sated, seek new ecstasies.
Keep to the caves
or hide in olive groves
when ships sail your way.

Carmen

I'm the "no name woman" now,
but you can read the story.
They changed the names, but not the reality.
I hope your story ends well. Mine did not.

Love is a wayward bird. It cannot be tamed.
It flies, goes where it wants to go.
Follow love wherever it leads you
but beware. When a gypsy or any other woman
tempts a man he falls under a spell.

Luring men into disaster,
as was my nature, always ends badly.
So when he stabbed me,
jealous and yelling my name
I deserved my fate.

Part Three

Alice Toklas

I heard bells. I looked at Gertrude
and heard bells ringing. She was golden,
glints in her hair, an aura surrounding her.
Big, heavy, with tiny hands.

I worked my way into her life.
I learned to type and every day typed
the words she wrote the night before.
I dusted the precious porcelain.

I was "Pussy" and she was "Lovey."
I cooked—roast turkey, apple pies,
lemon pies. I grew more adventurous later—
chicken-liver omelettes, truffles and Madeira wine.

I talked to the women. Gertrude talked to the men.
I started our summer garden in Bilignin,
planted an orchard, spent an hour every morning
picking berries for breakfast.

They wheeled her into the operating room.
I never saw her again. I had to practice economies.
Often cold and hungry, I prayed to Saint Francis.
I am buried in the tomb next to Gertrude.

Bonnie Parker

Clyde and me strolling down a back street
in some crummy town, looking all around,
sizing up the chances and then BAM!
"Quick, babe, that one,"
him pointing to a dusty black rattletrap,
and quick as can be we were in it,
rolling down the road singing "Not much money,
oh, but honey, ain't we got fun."

Nights, squeezed together on the back seat,
him fumblin', squeezin' me, buckin'
and rockin' and then, inside me bursting like the sun rising.

I loved the way my heart raced, loved the wind whipping my
hair,
hearing Clyde shout, "Let's get rolling."
He was powerful when he bounced around in the driver's seat,
raced the car around curves, pounding on the steering wheel,
howling like a wolf in heat.

Truth be told, that's when he let go, let the wild boy
inside him take over. Not so good with his moves otherwise,
you know what I mean, better behind the wheel than in bed,

but fun is fun wherever you catch it.

Empress Alexandra

My mother ruined my life. There, I've said it and I'm glad.
Mama, a tyrant of the worst sort,
looked like a loving mother for photographs,
embraced us as we sat around her dressed in those
fussy clothes so we could never play like other children.

We had to do the proper walk, the proper smile,
read the proper books. Even in Balmoral never joy,
never free to run through glens, to crawl in heather
looking for deer. Always walking in pairs down the
same paths, always dreary prayers from sour parsons.

I loved Nicki. But his mother was a demon,
worse than mine! Disaster followed disaster,
the final horror the arrival of drunken dirty men
smelling like a slaughterhouse, shouting curses,
prodding us with rough, blood-stained hands,

yanking us off trains into cold, filthy cottages.
Then pushing, prodding us with clubs and knives, until
Yekaterinburg, where the chief of our guard
screamed, "Let them go to hell!"

When those hairy rebels forced us into a basement
and shot us it ended my misery. I was praying
for God to admit me to His court in Heaven
where I might be safe and loved.
But I am in a mob of cruel-looking people,

the thieves, robbers, fallen women here
crying "Misère, misère!" as did my mother.
I am no better than they. I did not deserve
our luxuries or appreciate good fortune.

Ethel Rosenberg

The Feds will never catch us, we said to each other, and the thrill
of getting deeper and deeper into secret channels added a frisson
to lovemaking. Julius was my Caesar and I submitted in all ways.
We were never closer than those days we worked together.

For us it was a holy war.
America had become a tool of big business,
crushing the working people, enslaving the poor,
exalting the power and dominance of fascists.

Julius was the top man, and I was so proud
to be a team, decoding messages, meeting agents,
raising money. Always looking over our shoulders.
We could bring the Party forward, for peace.

We were so careful. Meetings secret, recruits carefully vetted.
We laughed at the "flat foots" sure to bungle our case.
In the end, at Sing Sing, in my green-and-white polka-dotted dress,
I sat on the chair and said, "I have nothing to say. I'm ready."

Eva Braun

He married me the night before the last big conflagration,
said the fires, flames, hallowed our union, that we would emerge
from the ruins sanctified, cleansed, the god
and goddess of a new holy nation.

He gloried in what he called our Götterdämmerung.
We would rise from the ashes victorious, the enemies
had thrown the last roll of the dice, their planes
and pilots, consumed by the heat, smoke, fires,
perish in the battle drawn to death by their own vengeance.
He believed when we emerged from the bunker we would see an
exhausted world ready for us and we would rule that world
forever.

As the building swayed, crumbled, glass and plaster,
bricks and wooden beams crashed, fell, he began screaming,
raised his fist to the ceiling, trembled,
swayed, snatched his gun from his pocket,
fired it, shuddered, slumped, and fell.
I saw his soul go straight to hell, enter the steaming pit.

I closed my eyes as the flames approached,
swallowed the pill and surrendered myself.

Florence Ballard

"Supreme?" There was nothing supreme about my life.
Every time I stood up, tried, I got knocked down.
You don't think so? How about fifteen kids living
in squalid public housing? My father dying
while I was still young? How about being raped at sixteen?
How about being pushed aside so Diana Ross could sing lead?

You'd fall in love with booze if your life was like that.
'Specially if Motown Records worked behind your back,
"covering" for you in case you'd gotten so drunk
you couldn't stand, sway and sing. 'Specially if they paid you
peanuts.
'Specially if your husband left you and the kids,
and your house was foreclosed when you were just getting your
grip,
reconciling with Diana, some recognition at last,
and then BAM! A blood clot hits your heart and you're a goner.

Supreme? Hah! Don't make me laugh.

Francesca di Rimini

One day alone, we read of Lancelot and Guinevere.
Like Guinevere, I knew that love consumes the lover.
Paolo was my husband's brother. Our love was forbidden
but his hand touched mine as he turned the page.
I felt a surge of passion. He did too. I saw it in his eyes.
We kissed and felt the flames of longing.
The sweet desire we felt and the gentle caressing
we gave freely lifted us from dreary duty of our marriage beds
and became a sacred union that gave us ecstasy.
Death brought us release from earthly constraints.
Gently judged, we were not sent to the flames.
Our sin was lust. Now, embracing, we whirl in circles
clinging to one another, sighing. Our hearts filled with love,
we celebrate eternity embracing.

Heloise

I thrilled to Euclid: "A point is that which has no part."
Who knew that before he wrote those magic words?
or "The whole is greater than the part."
I imagined Socrates sitting in his tunic, one slipper dangling,
saying, "An unexamined life is not worth living."
Aristotle left me cold, he had a lawyer's mind, setting down the
rules,
but concede he was right in saying, "All virtue is summed up
in dealing justly."
I became an addict. The words "Patrologia Latinae" moved me
as no lute or harp when Abelard and I read
in the dim rooms along the Rue Clovis.

He plucked the fruit from the tree of knowledge, and I bit,
then chewed and swallowed.
Zeno, Heraclitus, Pythagoras, our world was governed by num-
bers,
and so, harmonious.
Athenagoras, Polycarp, Origen, Seneca, I whispered the names
while peeling apples.
I felt like a queen as I brushed my hair,
wishing to read their words forever.
Abelard opened my mind to Al-Kindi, who studied the heavens
and made perfumes from musk and amber.

Pride led me astray. The young counts from Anjou
would own the world, talking to kings and speaking of meta-
physics.
I was doomed, I thought, to manage a castle, entertain the count-
esses
with polite conversation while my brain
bubbled with proofs of God's existence.
So when he seduced me, I saw it as the path to freedom.
But I was not a nobleman free to choose my own life.
Silly woman! I chose freedom and got notoriety.

Josephine Baker

I used my body more than I should have.
My banana belt was a sensation. I knew what I was doing.
Crazed by the music pulsing in my body,
no longer the little not-black not-white girl
from St. Louis. No more deference to Whitey. I freed myself.
I loved France.

On the same earth
where people danced all night, drank, worshipped money,
children were searching for food in trash.
I treasured every child
I could help, mothered them, with a love I never
felt for the men I dallied with. God knows what I did,
and that's all that matters.

Josephine Bonaparte

I should have known Napoleon would find out. Should have known
he would never feel the same. In his eyes he had lost power over me.
I should have known he would turn to another woman.
Above all, his needs drove him.
"Power is my mistress," he said. Then I found him
with my lady-in-waiting. He'd got even in the love game.

As much for show as anything, he crowned me
after he crowned himself,
shocking the Pope and the notables. But being always bent on
breaking rules was how he kept us in thrall.
"What will he do next?" we asked ourselves.
So we were all were on edge.

It wasn't long before I could not give him a child.
So it had to be my fault.
He desperately wanted an heir to carry his name, his plans.
The crown meant nothing to me. I longed for attention, devotion.
I was shuffled off to a chateau in the countryside when Marie Louise,
his new wife/plaything, took my place. Good luck to her, I thought,
wondering how long she would last; not long.
He'd find someone new.
He learned of my death in his exile. He told any listener
that he truly loved me. He loved only himself and power.

Lucretia Borgia

That's my first husband's tomb over there
beneath the fig tree.
O mio caro, how I miss him.
But he gorged himself on mushrooms.
Every day he searched my garden.
Then he said, "Cara, prego, pollo con funghi,"
and I prepared the dish myself,
not trusting the cook.
I sliced the tender flesh and braised it in wine,
added a dash of olive oil to sweeten it.
My hands only, so I thought,
ladling the sauce.
One night, when he took a breath, strained
and rolled his eyes,
I thought he was teasing me, saying, "So hard I have to work to
savor this."
The doctor said, on examining his entrails,
he had consumed such an amount
of poison it could have killed an elephant.
But he did not know my Giovanni.
He could have eaten all the mushrooms in Umbria
and still kept eating.

The tomb of my second husband, Alfonso,
is in the crypt of the chapel.
He roamed the forests and
like a goat, scrambled among the shale
and scurried in the bracken.
Once, he brought back hemlock he had found
and scattered it near my garden.
I did not want it among my precious plants.
Cutting open his beautiful body,
the doctors said some evil traces, hemlock or monkshood
might have secured his demise.
There was some method there, I tell you.

Lorena Hickok

You won't see me in photos of Franklin and Eleanor.
Every single photo, from the campaign trail or at a conference,
has been cropped. I might have been standing next to her
but there's no sign of me, who held her many a night.
I shared a bed with Eleanor at Hyde Park and in the White
House.
Not bad for a poor girl from Bowdle, South Dakota,
with a "cover" job at Federal Emergency Relief,
arranged so I could be near. And near her I was.
Nights when she in her pink nightgown and me
in my blue silk Sulka pajamas would wrap our arms,
our legs around each other, our kisses lasted till dawn.
And then Eleanor moved out of my bed and my life.
Now I'm just one more fat broad lookin' for another lover.

Madame Chiang Kai-Shek

We write our own destiny. We become what we do.
I was a flower. Surrounding me were rocks,
fierce mountains, turbulent streams.
My way was to rise, tall and strong.

Life gave me a sturdy reed
to cling to—General Chiang.
The path he walked became my path.
I was the wind that swept aside our enemies
with charm, smiles, gracious bows,
soft words lulling those who would master us.

Another reed grew among us—
Mister Willkie. Looking in his eyes
I saw a will to break our foes.

As a bear is captured by the hint of honey
in one brief night I enslaved him.
Like a carp caught in a net, he struggled and succumbed.
I said I would follow him,
create of him a great leader.

I was foiled by his friend, my enemy
who forced me to watch the burning of my empire.
I raked my talons into his face
to scar him.
Time would tell. The friend, the enemy
fell from power. I rose.

Part Four

Princess Margaret Rose

I was the young
and pretty, witty princess
and Elizabeth the serious and dull one.

Young, rich blades were said to be in love with me.
Every week the papers published
a "Princess Pursued" story.

Rubbish. I loved to flirt, to pet,
to be the most popular girl in the kingdom
because life in our family was so boring.
Then I was the ensnaring, rapacious girl
out to lure a man into romance and marriage.

I met Peter Townsend and thinking
I knew what love was, let him charm me
and croon about becoming my husband.

Horrified I might marry a commoner,
my parents set the government and Church,
the public and the papers, against us.

Tony stepped right up, cast himself as my rescuer.
Whatever his "inclinations," he was not shy
about seizing the moment and me.

I admit I became a shrew, a lush, a bad mother,
an embarrassment to the government, the country.
What was I to do? Fade away?

Marilyn Monroe

Each person had his own "Marilyn."
Take your pick. I wasn't any of them, not inside.
I was everyone's idea of what I was and none of that was me.

The trouble was and is I don't know who I was.
I've had a lot time lately to try to figure it out.
Maybe one day I'll let you know, if I feel like it.

Marion Davies

Honey, let me tell you it was no bed of roses.
That old man was a drag. If it wasn't one thing,
it was entertain his old fuddy-duddy guests
at that monstrous castle in the foggy hills; way,
way out in No-wheres-ville, California,
or vamoose when that old battle-axe,
Mrs. William Randolph Hearst, if you please,
decides she wants to swan all over the place
with her friends. Then I have to haul my ass
down to L.A. or up to San Francisco. She snaps
her fingers and little Willie bows and scrapes
to keep the peace. I think she hates the castle
and sashays in and out just to rattle our cages.

I know I gotta stop griping, after all I was a chorus girl
from Brooklyn, not born rolling in dough.
But give me a break, I made enough money
to keep my family in clover. And did they love it.
I worked my butt off, three movies a year,
sparking with Willie, smiling, showing my tits,
and bailed him out with a million bucks
to save him from bankruptcy. That's what a girl has gotta do.

Yeah, in the end, scotches at noon
and wine got me through those deadly
LaDeAh folks who sponged off us at meal time.

He came through, left me 170,000 shares
of Hearst Corporation stock so it's not as though I wasted my
time.

Mary, Queen of Scots

Was any queen as tormented by grief, treachery
and death as I? Six days old I was when Father
died and from that day my life was one of sorrow.
Too much happened too soon.
Shipped off to France, married to the Dauphin,
he died a year later. Trundled back to Scotland,
I married Darnley. Two years and he was killed
in an explosion in the castle.
Then faster than an eagle can fly, married to Bothwell,
forced from my throne. Imprisoned eighteen years
by my wretched cousin Elizabeth, moved from one horrible
prison to another, I pleaded for mercy all the while, longing
to see my son. He succeeded me on the Scottish throne,
sending not a word before I was beheaded after
twenty years a captive.

Did I ever have a happy day? Did I ever feel a son's love,
was I ever lavished with caresses from a man, was I enchanted
by a love song, a stroll hand in hand in a garden? No, and no
and no.

Mata Hari

My body stocking and jeweled bra:
They worked. Men pursued me.
To draw more lovers into my web I played a role.
A mistake. The game was bigger than I realized.

I shouldn't have been playing
on a field that wasn't mine.
There I stood, twelve men facing me.
They gripped their rifles. I stared at them.
"I will not wear a blindfold,
I want to see the sky brightening."

I did not spy against France.
I only wanted to play act. I only wanted money.
Why would I spy? What would it achieve?
Sex was more my style, not skullduggery.

The darkness was comforting as I stood there
but I saw faint streaks of light in the sky
so I knew the moment was near.
The men shifted from one foot to the other.

I think they wished it were all over.
I was not afraid. I knew there would be pain
for a second and then nothing, a release.
Ah, they raised their rifles.
Someone had given a silent signal.

Sally Hemings

My Lord, what mourning! Miss Martha and then
the little children. Was there ever so much sorrow
in this world than the afflictions visited on this family?
The master, Mister Jefferson, weighted down
with grief and woe, wandered alone in the gardens,
riding his horse aimlessly in the wood.
It did break my heart to see him so.

I heard "Abide with Me" and my tears started flowing,
like a river, a river of love for this family.
So I did what any woman would do.
I consoled him, sang to him, cradled him,
wiped away his tears. That man, he did know how to love
and I gave love when it was needed.

Salome

He leaned toward me, panting.
He could hardly say the words,
"Ask of me whatever you want."
I wanted to ask for a night of love,
but dared not with my mother watching.

She pulled me aside. I know she knew
what I wanted. Her face contorted with hate,
she said, "Ask for the head of John,"
who said her marriage
was unlawful. If I disobeyed, her wrathful
harangues would echo in the palace.
So I said, "The head of John, on a platter."

Swiftly it was done, and his head, the hair matted with dirt,
his beard encrusted with bread crumbs
and honey, his eyes staring as if to say
"Forever you will be known as a foul woman,"
was laid before Herod, who turned to
my mother, and grimaced as if to say
"Are you satisfied now, you shrew?"

John's beheading satisfied not
my lust for Herod, not my mother's
fury, and Herod, instead of seducing me,
shrank at the sight of me.

Sappho

Never again,
never again.

I will never again suffer
the capture of my soul.

A memory of you
standing staring at me,
the sun over your shoulder
bathing you in honey.

One kiss, that was all.

Virginia Woolf

Vita's voice, soothing like a mother's,
coaxing like a lover's, enchanted me. Guiding me,
she gestured to the fields in the distance.
"One day, we will walk through those fields
and never return." Later, in her bed high in the tower
of Sissinghurst, she said we would escape our dreary London lives,
run away as she had done before. A new life, I thought,
and clung to her.

She would save me from the tedium of laying out pages,
rescue me from demands of family and routine and Leonard's
fussing.
Escaping to the south of France, to a tumbled-down bastide,
we could live there, love, write all the words locked inside us.
Of course love is a wanderer, floating away like the clouds
on a summer's eve. Slowly, like a leaf floating from a branch,
Vita disappeared, leading another lover down the avenue of lime
trees.

I lived with the pain for years. War and the loneliness of life
broke my heart. One day I took my stick from the corner
 by the cottage door, walked through fields to the swing bridge
at Southease—a lovely word, Southease.
"I shall end it now," I thought as I walked into the river.
The water surged around me. I felt lifted.
Sinking I willed myself to stay under.

Wallis, Duchess of Windsor

Darlings, I know you think it was glamorous.
The French Riviera, Paris, New York City, diamonds,
emeralds, sables, Chanel, Jacques Fath, Faberge,
all that glitter. Dining with those divine men—
Ari Onassis, Gianni Agnelli, Ali Khan.

But my little man, as I called him (and believe me,
he was little where it counts), was tedious.
That family, how they ever managed to rule a country,
obsessed with horses, hunting, tramping through heather.
Had he ever read a book, listened to an opera?

It wasn't as if we had money. I mean real money,
not what the finance minister doled out.
Thank God our friends who understood the situation
were grateful for the publicity. But it was pitiful
that his brothers sat in their castles, waited on hand and foot.

I never set out to be Queen. He believed I would be "accepted."
I never doubted they would drive him off the throne
and blame me. I never loved him. Yes, I "took care of him,"
aroused him with my special skills, cooed at him
to keep up his spirits, but never, ever thought he would cling so.
And he did cling.

Whitney Houston

I slipped beneath the water that night. So easy.
I'm lonely here where smoke is swirling,
people are plodding, thirsting, noisy,
horrible heat and when I try to sing no sound comes out.

A while ago, I can't remember when,
I sang "When I'm racing with destiny…"
and when I remembered the words
"… I will face eternity" I cried out because this is eternity.

I sang "The Greatest Love of All" but no love here.
I, who topped the Billboard albums charts,
nominated for Album of the Year. Great love isn't happening
and I long for a touch, a kiss, a smile.

If I could do it again, would I do it the same way?
Probably. I was an ordinary girl from New Jersey
who happened to have a great voice and wanted fame.

Zelda Fitzgerald

There's no booze. At this time of night,
in Paris, Scott and I drank a few glasses
of scotch or gin at home and moved on to Le Select or
La Rotonde, had a drink or two with Ernest or Dos,
then dinner and more drinks at La Closerie des Lilas.

It's boring here, wandering, no drink in hand,
none of our drinking buddies in sight. I crave a pastis
or a glass or two (or three) of champagne
but there's no bartender. I'm in Nowhere land.

People say I wrecked Scott's career,
said he had written the greatest novel
ever, but, honey chile, that bluenose bundle
of nerves couldn't get started
without a "morning-pick-me-up" and a bottle by his desk.

People read the words Scott stole from me.
Books about me, dead but not forgotten,
give me a lovely shiver.

About the Author

Gail Marshall graduated from Marymount Manhattan College where Joseph P. Clancy, a poet and translator of Welsh poetry, encouraged her work, and from Washington University in St. Louis. For many years she was on the editorial board of *Education and Information Technology*, a publication sponsored by Information and Educational Technology, a working group affiliated with UNESCO.

www.ingramcontent.com/pod-product-compliance
Lightning Source LLC
Chambersburg PA
CBHW031209160726
47992CB00006B/2650